SydneyAustralia

SydneyAustralia
JimCromarty

Destinations: Sydney, Australia

© copyright 2007 Jim Cromarty

ISBN: 978-1-84550-234-8

1-84550-234-5

Published by Christian Focus Publications Ltd, Geanies House,

Fearn, Tain, Ross-shire, IV20 1TW, Scotland, Great Britain.

www.christianfocus.com

email:info@christianfocus.com

Cover design by Danie van Straaten

Cover illustration: The Sydney Opera House

Maps by Fred Apps.

Photographs available from Ablestock unless otherwise credited.

Printed and Bound in Denmark

by Norhaven Paperback A/S.

www.christianfocus.com

CONTENTS

SYDNEY TODAY

The city of Sydney started its life as one big prison - the fashionable place in the 1700s to send the average criminal from the United Kingdom. So in 1988 they decided to celebrate the fact that Sydney was now 200 years old - but no longer part of a penal colony.

Sydney began on 26 January 1788 when Governor Arthur Phillip arrived with convicts to establish the colony. Sydney is Australia's largest city, is 17,200 km from London, 16,100 km from New York and 7,850 km from Tokyo. These distances don't prevent tourists taking a holiday in Australia, and each year Sydney attracts several million visitors.

Most countries have towns of which its inhabitants are proud, but many of these are not well known to the rest of the world. However, Sydney is world famous. For a start it was chosen to host the Olympic Games in 2000. When Sydney is mentioned today most people either think of that or they think of the Sydney Harbour Bridge, the Opera House and the magnificent harbour. But there is a lot more to Sydney as we shall find out: History; People; Architecture; Wild life and Faith.

Sydney was made a city in 1842. It was named after Thomas Townsend who was Viscount Sydney, the Secretary of State for the British Colonies at the time. At first the colony had 1,455 people and it was not until 1925 that the population reached one million. In 1963 there were two million people living there and in 2005 the population was approximately five million.

Following the discovery of gold in the 1850s many migrants came to Australia hoping to make their fortune. Some did, but most ran out of money and made their way to Sydney and other towns looking for work. Following World War II Australia opened its doors and many hundreds of thousands of displaced people came here to start a new life. Sydney's population grew quickly as many found work in the rapidly expanding urban regions. There are over one hundred different nationalities living in the city of Sydney, and these people speak more than twenty different languages.

In recent years many people from the war torn Middle East have come to Australia to start a new life. There are a lot of things to sort out when people come into a new culture and country. Sydney, like all modern cities has its fair share of modern-day problems. But on the plus side Sydney has a wonderful climate and on average there are only thirty-two days each year when the sun doesn't shine. The warm weather and golden sandy beaches mean that surfing is very popular in both summer and winter.

The Sydney Harbour (Port Jackson) is a safe place for large ships. At its entrance the water depth is just over twenty-four metres and elsewhere averages nine metres. Within the harbour the shore stretches for about 250 kilometres and outside the Heads, to the north and south there is almost sixty kilometres of beaches. Port Jackson has an area of fifty-five square kilometres which means that there is plenty of room for thousands of small boats and large ships to move about. Each weekend many 'weekend' sailors are in their boats, their sails a kaleidoscope of bright colours.

Sydney is well known for its sports. Football, cricket, tennis, golf and a host of other games are played each week.

Some time ago I read a description of Sydney by a woman who had moved there to live. She wrote:

'Sydney's fantastic... At first I was lonely - I'd left home for the first time and here I was in this vast city. But now I find everywhere else boring.... I try to do everything.

'There is horse-riding in the outer west, Rugby Union in the winter months and the beach in summer.

'I love all water sports and Sydney's just great with its beaches and the harbour. I love picnics and every week I find a new place. I think the big thing about Sydney is going out and being out. Maybe there's bad things but I just don't see them ... I'm so busy seeing the good things.'

Sydney is growing quickly. Houses are being built in new subdivisions and mansions worth many millions of dollars line the harbour shores. Maybe one day you'll visit Sydney and see some of them.

Whilst Sydney is built by human hands, the Bible tells us of another city, the city of God which has been prepared by God as the dwelling place of every Christian.

You might remember how God called Abraham to go to the land of Canaan which would one day become home for his descendants. He was overjoyed with God's promise, but he looked for something much better. We read in the Bible: 'By faith Abraham obeyed when he was called to go out to the place which he would receive as an inheritance.... By faith he dwelt in the land of promise as in a foreign country, dwelling in tents with Isaac and Jacob, the heirs with him of the same promise; for he waited for the city which has foundations, whose builder and maker is God' (Hebrews 11:8-10). All Christians long for their eternal home, built by the Lord Jesus, their Saviour. He told his disciples: 'In my Father's house are many mansions; if it were not so, I would have told you. I go to prepare a place for you. And if I go and prepare a place for you, I will come again and receive you to myself; that where I am, there you may be also' (John 14:2-3).

Jesus didn't build these homes with a hammer and nails, but by his death on the cross and his perfect obedience to his Heavenly Father. This he did in the place of his people. The New Jerusalem, as the Bible calls the Christian's home, will be found in the new heavens and new earth. It will be perfect in every way and there will be nothing which will cause fear. God will be with his people 'and he will wipe away every tear from their eyes; there shall be no more death, nor sorrow, nor crying. There shall be no more pain, for the former things have passed away' (Revelation 21:4).

The best dwelling place of all will be God's Heavenly Jerusalem.

A WHISTLE-STOP TOUR OF AUSTRALIA

Some Basic Facts

Australia is 7, 686, 848 square kilometres in size.
From east to west it measures 3, 983 kilometres,
and from north to south, 3, 138 kilometres. The
coastline measures 27, 948 kilometres which
includes Tasmania and the 821 small islands
dotted along Australia's coastline.

Australia's highest mountain is Mount
Kosciusko which is 2,228 metres above sea level.

In Australia most people live along the coastal
plains where the rainfall is sufficient to support
the population and provide adequate water to
grow the crops needed to support life. In 2002 the
population of Australia was estimated to be close
to 20, 000, 000.

GUILTY!

The nation of Great Britain had a problem - her prisons and gaols were overflowing with men and women who had been convicted of committing a great variety of crimes. This overcrowding caused criminals to be locked up in the rotting ships that were anchored along the Thames River. In an effort to overcome the problem of housing the convicts, many of the worst criminals were transported to North America.

When the USA gained her independence, the British Government decided to transport criminals to Australia or 'The Land Down Under' which in

1770 had been claimed by Captain James Cook for the British crown. The convicts would be well out of the way and would work to build a settlement where timber for ship building could be easily obtained. It was believed that the timber in New South Wales and Norfolk Island was better and stronger than anything found in Great Britain or Europe.

Many of the criminals housed in the ship hulks had been sentenced to death, sometimes for minor crimes such as stealing food for their starving families, but this was changed to lengthy gaol sentences in Australia. Many of these had their death sentence commuted to 7, 14 or 21 years.

A fleet of eleven British ships, under the command of Governor Arthur Phillip was assembled for the 25,000 kilometre journey to Australia. The fleet sailed from Plymouth Harbour in May, 1787. On board were 759 convicts (both men and women), 252 marines with their wives and children, 20 officials, 210 seamen, 233 merchants and 13 children of the convicts. Those sailing ships carried not only people, but all the food that was needed for the journey and sufficient for meals until the colony was self-supporting.

Three ships were filled with supplies. Someone said they were like floating farms. It was necessary to bring cows for meat and milk as well as pigs, horses and sheep, as none of these animals were to be found in Australia. With all the animals on board, those ships must have looked like Noah's ark. Bags of seeds were stacked away so that crops could be grown in the new country. Some people brought along their pet dogs and cats while others had their pet rabbits with them.

Life was difficult on the ships. There was little space and the convicts were locked up below deck for most of the journey. When a convict broke the Governor's laws he was severely punished.

One very cruel punishment was whipping with 'the cat of nine tails' which was a whip of nine knotted leather strips. After the whipping it was usual to rub salt into the wounds to help the healing, but the salt caused the open wounds to sting more than ever. Despite the hardships on board only thirty-two people died during the nine months at sea.

On 18th January, 1788 the First Fleet arrived at Botany Bay, just south of Port Jackson but it wasn't the ideal place for a settlement - the water in the bay was shallow and the ships were open to the strong north easterly winds that blew most days. The settlers found the land to be too sandy and marshy for a settlement to succeed. As there was little fresh water in the region, the fleet moved north along the coast to Sydney Cove (Port Jackson) where the landing was made on 26 January, 1788.

The Union Jack was raised and the soldiers fired a volley of shots while Governor Phillip formally took possession of the land. The Australian aborigines living there at that time had no say in the matter, and the land they loved became the possession of Great Britain.

The wide, deep harbour was ideal for the ships, and fresh water was found in a stream running into the harbour. It was claimed that Sydney Harbour was capable of providing sufficient space for at least 1,000 sailing ships.

Soon the convicts, many having their legs chained together were taken ashore. The worst criminals had an iron ball attached to the chain making escape impossible, and all were guarded by well armed soldiers. Australia was a perfect gaol. Being an island, escape by sea was impossible. Escape into the bush meant the fear of being speared by the natives, or simply starving to death.

Life was hard for everyone, especially the convicts, but they had broken the law and were being punished.

To break God's law - that is to 'sin' - means judgement. We read in the Bible: 'The wages of sin is death...' (Romans 6:23). You might think that many of the punishments handed out to the convicts were cruel, but remember that the punishment for breaking God's law is death, both of the body and then the second death which is everlasting punishment. Some convicts returned home when they gained their freedom, but there is no possible escape from God's final punishment.

There is only one way to escape the wages of sin and that is by asking God to forgive you of your sins and then by trusting the Lord Jesus for your salvation. He lived and died so that his people might live with him forever. I pray that you love God and are saved by our Saviour, Jesus.

Many convicts said life in Australia was hell on earth. However, God's hell is to be feared much more than anything that happens in this world. To be saved by Jesus Christ is to be delivered from such a terrible end. I trust you are a Christian and will spend your everlasting life with the Lord Jesus and all of his people.

A WHISTLE-STOP TOUR OF AUSTRALIA

Into the Outback

The land beyond the Great Dividing Range is The Australian Outback. Uluru, one of the best known sites of the Australian outback is also called Ayers Rock. It was the homeland of the Pitjantjatjara and Yankunytjatjara people and is now listed as a World Heritage site.

Ayers Rock was seen by the explorer, William Gosse in 1873 and named after the then Premier of South Australia, Sir Henry Ayers. In 1995 it was returned to its original aboriginal owners.

This huge rock is 9.4 kilometres in circumference, 3.6 kilometres in length and 2 kilometres wide. It is made of arkosic sandstone and is 345 metres high.

WATER!

As soon as the convicts arrived in Australia they were set to work clearing the trees and scrub, erecting tents for Governor Phillip, for soldiers, marines and free men, fencing areas for the cattle and preparing the land for planting seeds. The convicts often worked in chains guarded by armed soldiers who made sure they carried out their duties and didn't try to escape.

Running through the settlement was a stream of fresh water which was given the name 'Tank Stream.' This fresh water was essential for the survival of the people and animals. The local aborigines and native animals used the creek for their fresh water. The animals muddied the once clear water, but it had to be used by everyone.

No doubt some of the convicts had to carry water from the Tank Stream to water the newly sown seeds. Others would have had to keep troughs filled for the animals that were fenced in to prevent them escaping into the bush. Some convicts kept barrels and tanks filled for the soldiers, sailors, the free men and convicts. Water from the stream would have been used for bathing and washing clothes.

The Tank stream still exists, although it can't be seen by people who are walking the streets of Sydney today. The stream has had its bed and sides cemented and tall buildings and roadways cover it.

Water is essential to life. Without it we would die within a few days. The Lord Jesus spoke about water many times. On one occasion he met a Samaritan woman while he was waiting beside Jacob's well (John 4:1-26). His disciples had gone into the city of Sychar to buy some food. This woman had come to the well to fill her container. She was surprised when Jesus asked her for a drink, as normally the

Jews had nothing to do with the Samaritans. Jesus offered her 'living water' to drink. He said that to drink the water he offered would satisfy her thirst for ever. She really wanted that water as she thought she'd never again have to go to Jacob's well to get it. Jesus was however speaking of salvation and the Holy Spirit who is God and lives within the hearts of all of his followers.

On another occasion, Jesus was in Jerusalem for the Feast of Tabernacles. This was when Jews celebrated their escape from Egypt and their arrival at the Promised Land. During their long journey they had lived in tents. The Israelites celebrated this memory by making little huts to live in on the tops of their houses. They would then remember how God had cared for them during that time. It was a happy feast. It must have been great fun for the children - like living in a 'cubby house.'

On the last day of that feast Jesus spoke to the crowds that had gathered: 'If anyone thirsts, let him come to me and drink. He who believes in me, as the Scripture has said, "out of his heart will flow rivers of living water." But this he spoke concerning the Spirit, whom those believing in him would receive...' (John 7:37-39).

Just as the Tank Stream provided fresh water which kept the people and animals alive, so also the Holy Spirit makes people spiritually alive. You must go to Jesus, repent of your sins and ask for the Holy Spirit to come into your heart. Then you will have eternal life - you will be a citizen of God's Kingdom.

A WHISTLE-STOP TOUR OF AUSTRALIA

Kangaroos

In Australia there are over sixty different varieties of kangaroo. The biggest of these animals are known as 'Big Red' and get their nickname because of the reddish fur of the male. The male can grow up to 1.8 metres in height and weigh ninety kilograms; the female has a different smoky-blue colouring and can be 1.25 metres in height and weigh up to thirty-five kilograms. Kangaroos being marsupials carry their young in a pouch. The total population of kangaroos in Australia is estimated to be about fifty million.

DESTINATIONS

FOOD SHORTAGES

Sydney, at the time of the settlement, was a land of bush and thick grass which had to be cleared so that tents could be erected. Most convicts knew they would never see their families and friends again as England was over 25,000 kilometres away. Because of the drought, food was in short supply and had to be rationed. It was also several years before ships arrived from Great Britain with more supplies and convicts.

Because of the shortage of food there were very strict laws about stealing. Just one month after the settlement had been made, four young convicts were caught stealing food from the supply tent. They were tried and found guilty. Two were banished from the settlement which meant they were possibly killed by the aborigines or starved to death; one was sentenced to 300 lashes from the dreaded 'cat of nine tails,' and the fourth was sentenced to death by hanging. Another convict was ordered to be the hangman, but when he refused to kill the frightened young convict, he was told he would be shot for refusing orders. When a soldier raised his rifle, the trembling convict put the noose about the thief's neck and the dreadful deed was done.

The convicts worked hard to build a town along the shores of Sydney Harbour. Some dug the soil and planted seeds in order to grow food for the future. There were no tractors as we have today to prepare the land for planting. Because of the drought, water was carried to the gardens to keep the plants alive. Other convicts dug wells to provide fresh water.

The soldiers often made their way through the bush to find kangaroos which they shot and ate.

However, for some years food was in short supply and many had little to eat.

A shortage of food to keep the body alive is terrible, but there is a hunger which is good for us. Jesus says in Matthew 5:6 'Blessed are those who hunger and thirst for righteousness, for they shall be filled.'

The prophet Amos wrote of another drought: "'Behold, the days are coming," says the Lord GOD, "That I will send a famine on the land, not a famine of bread, nor a thirst for water, but of hearing the words of the LORD. They shall wander from sea to sea, and from north to east; they shall run to and fro, seeking the word of the LORD, but shall not find it'" (Amos 8:11-12). This terrible time came to pass. God's people turned away from their LORD and worshipped the false gods of the surrounding nations. Later when they wanted the truth it was not to be found.

What an awful thing it would be if we didn't have Bibles to know what God was saying to us. In some countries the Bible is banned and churches are closed. There is a famine of the word of God. In the western world Bibles are freely available and many homes have three or four copies of the Scriptures. Read your Bible, attend worship and pray to God.

Learn as much of the Scripture as you can because the day might come when Christianity is outlawed and we won't be allowed to own a Bible. Pray that you will never experience a famine of God's word. Each time you sit down to eat, thank God for the food on your plate. Also thank the Lord for your Bible. Its message is food for your soul.

BREAD

As we have said the colony was suffering drought and food was in short supply. Great Britain was transporting more convicts which made the food shortage more serious. One convict, James Ruse was granted his freedom - given a 'Ticket-of-leave'. He was the first convict to be given a small grant of land (2 acres) which he could farm. He married a female convict and was given several convicts to help him build a hut in which to live. The convicts assisted him to clear his land and prepare the soil for planting wheat seed which had been supplied by Governor Phillip. Ruse had been a farmer in

England before being sent to Sydney where he soon gained his freedom because of his good behaviour and hard work.

Crops generally were failing, and as the shortage of food became worse, lookouts were appointed by Governor Phillip, in the hope of spotting supply ships from England. Meanwhile there was great rejoicing when Ruse's farm produced almost 200 bushels of wheat and sixty bushels of barley and oats. Some seed had to be put aside for planting the next year, but the rest was milled to make flour. This meant bread was made from a local crop of wheat!

Wheat grows best in Australia's dry areas because too much rain causes wheat to develop 'rust' which spoils the seed. Sydney's drought conditions proved excellent for Ruse's crop. The rain that fell did so at the right time to make the crop the success it was.

Jesus used bread in one of his miracles when he fed some thousands of people using a few loaves of bread and several fish. This he did by performing a great miracle (John 6:5-14).

Later Jesus said: 'I am the bread of life. Your fathers ate the manna in the wilderness, and are dead. This is the bread which comes down from heaven, that one may eat of it and not die. I am the living bread which came down from heaven. If anyone eats of this bread, he will live forever; and the bread that I shall give is my flesh, which I shall give for the life of the world' (John 6:47-51).

Just as we need food to keep our bodies alive, so we must have spiritual food to keep our faith alive. The best spiritual food is reading the Scriptures daily, attending worship, praying and reading good Christian books. We must go to Jesus, confess our sins and ask for forgiveness. If we trust ourselves to him and his sacrifice for us on the cross, we will live forever in the new heavens and earth.

SHEEP

Another couple to help overcome the food shortage during the early days of settlement was Captain John Macarthur and his wife Elizabeth who purchased some merino sheep when their ship called at Cape Town on its way to Sydney. They commenced a very valuable sheep industry, especially with wool which was used to make clothing. They found a ready market for mutton.

Soon the small flock had grown - the drought conditions were good for sheep who suffered with 'foot rot' in wet seasons. Macarthur's lambs were looked after with much care, and with cross breeding the Australian Merino sheep produced some of the world's finest wool.

Later in the nineteenth century when the farmers and shepherds moved to the outback areas of Australia, they usually made an annual trip to Sydney to sell their farming produce. They would then buy sufficient food and other goods, to last for the following year. In the early days the bales of wool were packed on drays and pulled along to the markets by a team of strong bullocks. Now the wool is usually transported by rail.

Jesus had a lot to say about sheep. On several occasions he said: 'I am the good shepherd. The good shepherd gives his life for the sheep' (John 10:11).

When John the Baptist saw him approaching, asking to be baptised he said: 'Behold! The Lamb of God who takes away the sin of the world' (John 1:29).

Jesus was compared to the small lambs that were offered as sacrifices to God. Our Saviour would offer himself on the cross and there pay the penalty owed to God for the sins of his people.

Did Jesus pay the penalty for your sins?

If so then trust him, love him and follow him!

Try to learn the 23rd Psalm: 'The LORD is my shepherd; I shall not want. He makes me to lie down in green pastures; he leads me beside the still waters. He restores my soul; he leads me in the paths of righteousness for his name's sake.

'Yea, though I walk through the valley of the shadow of death, I will fear no evil; for you are with me; your rod and your staff, they comfort me. You prepare a table before me in the presence of my enemies; you anoint my head with oil; my cup runs over.

'Surely goodness and mercy shall follow me all the days of my life; and I will dwell in the house of the LORD forever.'

Is Christ, the Shepherd, your Saviour?

A WHISTLE-STOP TOUR OF AUSTRALIA

Koala

Contrary to popular belief, a Koala's fur is thick, not soft and cuddly. They have five fingers per paw with the first two as opposable thumbs, providing better gripping ability.

The Koala is a generally silent animal, but males have a very loud advertising call that can be heard from almost a kilometre away during the breeding season. The Koala lives almost entirely on eucalyptus leaves and spends a lot of its day resting. Koalas spend about three of their five active hours eating. An average Koala eats 500 grams of eucalyptus leaves each day, chewing them in its powerful jaws to a very fine paste before swallowing.

DESTINATIONS

PINCHGUT ISLAND

The colony at Sydney was really a gaol without walls. When laws were broken cruel punishment was frequently handed out, sometimes by ministers of religion who often acted as judges. Today in Sydney the punishment for crime is very lenient compared to the sentences handed down in the early days of the settlement.

On 12 April, 1790 Thomas Halford was found guilty of stealing about six kilograms of potatoes, worth one shilling and six pence. It was a time of food shortages and the judge decided to make the punishment a warning to anyone else who was thinking of stealing. He sentenced Halford to 2,000 lashes with the whip. This was an extremely harsh penalty! The usual punishment for theft was two to three hundred lashes often with the dreaded 'cat-o'-nine tails.'

This whip was very much like the whip the Romans used to abuse the Lord Jesus. Christ had come into the world to save his people, and part of that saving work was to be punished by God in the place of his sinful people. Before he was crucified on that Easter Friday the Roman soldiers tormented, abused and whipped the Lord. Many people died just by being whipped. It was a cruel thing that was done to our Lord and Saviour. If you are a Christian he paid the penalty for your sins. Daily you should thank the Lord for suffering hell in your place. The Bible tells us that God 'made him who knew no sin to be sin for us, that we might become the righteousness of God in him' (2 Corinthians 5:21). He took our sins and gave us his righteousness! What a loving Saviour.

It wasn't only the convicts who broke the colony's laws. Six marines who had been stealing food from the stores were paraded before the judge who sentenced them all to death by hanging.

Some found guilty of lesser crimes were punished with a whipping, while others were forced to wear a sign reading - 'Thief' or 'Rogue'! Some had to wear leg irons which made work very difficult. The iron clamps locked around their legs caused bruising and cut into the skin.

In the Sydney Harbour was a small island where the local aborigines caught good sized fish and the occasional shark. Governor Phillip realised that the island would be a perfect gaol for the worst lawbreakers. Escape was only possible by boat or the long swim through shark infested water.

The island soon became known as 'Pinchgut Island' as the convicts sentenced to spend a time there, lived on bread and water, with the result that their stomachs shrank. The island had another use - sometimes the bodies of convicted criminals who had been hung were taken to the island and hung on a gibbet. There they remained until their bones became white - the birds having feasted on their flesh.

Pinchgut Island, as a place of punishment, was greatly feared!

In 1857 the island became a fort to protect Sydney against a feared invasion by the Russian navy. The island was enlarged with 8,000 tonnes of sandstone carried there by boat. This made possible the building of a fort with three muzzle loading cannons. Thankfully they have never been fired in anger.

A WHISTLE-STOP TOUR OF AUSTRALIA

Fort Denison

This could be known as Sydney's Alcatraz as Fort Denison was built as a defensive facility. It occupies a small island located north of the Royal Botanical Gardens in Sydney Harbour. The island was originally named Pinchgut (see main chapter for possible reason). Its function was as a place of confinement for convicts during the early period of British settlement. The fortress was built in the mid 19th century as a defence against a feared Russian invasion during the Crimean War.

BUSHRANGERS

Australia's best known bushranger is Ned Kelly. He robbed many stagecoach travellers of their possessions, stole gold shipments and was guilty of murder. He proved very difficult to capture but eventually he and his gang were surrounded. Ned came out of hiding with a revolver in each hand and wearing a suit of tin with a slit in his mask so he could see. He was shot and after a trial, was hung. This didn't happen in Sydney, but Sydney can boast of having Australia's first bushranger.

This man was John Caesar, a Negro convict, with the nickname of 'Black Caesar.' He was a troublemaker right from the start. He worked hard, but continually stole food from others claiming that as he was such a big man he needed more food than he was given. Punishment was handed out, including being whipped, but he just laughed at the man doing the whipping, and usually made some smart remark when the whipping ended.

He was sent to Norfolk Island as punishment, but when he returned to Sydney, he escaped and joined a tribe of natives who at first welcomed him. However, he behaved so badly to the natives that they ended up having him speared. John then made his way back to Sydney to recover from his wounds. Then with the help of another convict, he stole some food and escaped into the bush. From his hideout in the dense scrub he continually stole from the settlers and became the most feared person in the Sydney area. 'Black Caesar' feared no one and was not afraid of death.

Finally the Governor offered five gallons of rum to the person who caught Caesar. In the early days of the Sydney settlement there was a shortage of money and people began using rum to pay their debts. This was to cause a lot of trouble later on.

On 14 February, 1796 a man named Wimbow

saw Caesar leaving his hideout. He waited for his chance and fired a shot which killed Australia's first bushranger.

How true are God's words 'The wages of sin is death!' (Romans 6:23) These are frightening words, but read on and you will find a wonderful promise '...the gift of God is eternal life in Christ Jesus our Lord.' We have a wonderful God!

A WHISTLE-STOP TOUR OF AUSTRALIA

The Emu

This is the second biggest bird in the world but it cannot fly. A fully grown emu can stand at 1.9 metres tall. Fully grown they can weigh up to forty-five kilograms. It has grey, brown feathers with small wings and long, strong legs. Each foot has three toes pointing forward. Along with the kangaroo it features on the Australian Coat of Arms. Both animals share the same characteristic of being unable to walk backwards. They therefore epitomise Australia's forward looking nature. Emu population numbers in Australia are estimated to be about 1 million. They make a loud booming noise using an air sack in their neck.

CHURCH SERVICES

The convicts weren't very interested in spiritual matters. There were no church services on board the ships sailing for Australia. Most convicts hated their English guards who handed out harsh punishment. Because the guards claimed to belong to the Church of England, their religion was also hated. A lot of the convicts were Irish Catholics who had rebelled against the Protestant British Government. They wanted nothing to do with the Church of England!

When the settlement was established at Sydney the first Church service was held on the 3rd of

February, 1788. The minister was the Rev Richard Johnson of the Church of England. It wasn't too long before ministers from other denominations arrived. A Methodist minister migrated to Sydney in 1815, and in 1820 an Irish priest arrived. As settlers moved away from Sydney the ministers had to travel many hundreds of miles on horseback to hold services. In those outback places a minister was seen possibly only once or twice a year.

Governor Phillip announced that convicts could marry, and within a few weeks of the settlement, fourteen convict couples did so.

The Church of England minister, Rev Johnson, pleaded with Governor Phillip to have a church built. However, it wasn't until 1793 that a building that could seat five hundred worshippers was opened. Rev Johnson personally met all the costs.

Governor Phillip gave Rev Johnson the help of two convicts, but only for two weeks. Mr Johnson paid them for the work they did. The payment was made in rum which the convicts thoroughly enjoyed!

The ministers knew that it was necessary to have a place to conduct worship. They understood the words of the Bible which said: 'Let us not give up meeting together, as some are in the habit of doing, but let us encourage one another...' (Hebrews 10:25 NIV).

The Presbyterians held their first services in the home of Dr Arndell, the godly James Mein leading worship. It was decided to build a hall and in 1809 a stone building was opened. Its walls were two feet thick and in 2006 it was still used for worship services.

In 1823 the Presbyterian Minister, John Dunmore Lang arrived in Sydney and spent many years encouraging settlers and ministers to come from Scotland. Mr Lang was responsible for the opening of some schools in Sydney and elsewhere.

Christianity has never been popular in Australia. Sunday is for most people, a day for sport, and the warm climate makes the beach very popular. On Sunday morning thousands make their way to the cool Sydney beaches with a surfboard on the car roof.

In parts of Sydney however, the name of the Lord Jesus Christ is glorified and church buildings are filled with Christians. Many people in country areas still attend worship despite small congregations. This land needs God to work in it.

A WHISTLE-STOP TOUR OF AUSTRALIA

The Jenolan Caves

In an area of Australia named The Blue Mountains there are the Jenolan Caves at Katoomba. You will be able to see Stalagmites and Stalactites. James McKeown is the first European to have discovered the caves. During the night native animals can be seen in the caves such as - the ring-tailed possum, sugar gliders, the boo book owl, wallabies and many more of God's creatures.

GOLD

Well behaved convicts were often given 'tickets of leave,' which meant they were given their freedom. Most were given grants of land to work. Farming eventually became a big business. With the wet seasons returning to the coastal regions, those involved in the sheep and wheat industry crossed the Great Dividing Range where they began working on large areas of land.

In the early years of settlement there were times when a convict found some small nuggets of gold. The officers feared that there would be an uprising by the convicts who would want to look for the precious metal. Usually the gold was confiscated and the convict punished for spreading the rumour that he'd found gold when it wasn't anything but 'fools' gold' - a metal that just looked like gold.

When gold was discovered in North America in the 1840s people from all over the world, including Australia set out to make their fortune. The Australian government decided that the time had come to find payable gold in Australia and offered a reward for the first person to make such a discovery. On 12 February, 1851 Edward Hargraves found gold near the township of Bathurst. The rulers of the nation knew that the discovery of gold would mean people coming to Australia in thousands - and this time they wouldn't be convicts but free men. These people would all be hoping to make a fortune mining on the gold fields.

Hargraves collected his reward and told his work mate: 'This is a memorable day in the history of New South Wales. I shall be a baronet, you will be knighted, and my old horse will be stuffed, put in a glass case, and sent to the British Museum.'

As a result of the gold discoveries, small townships sprang up in country areas, creating a greater need for food, which meant more farmers and shepherds were needed. In the meantime Sydney was growing in size, as unsuccessful gold miners made their way to the larger cities to find work.

Gold was a very valuable metal and overseas sales helped make Australia a wealthy nation.

Despite gold's value and scarcity we are told that in heaven the streets are paved with it (Revelation 21:21). Indeed when describing the new Jerusalem (heaven) the apostle John wrote: 'The construction of its wall was of jasper; and the city was pure gold, like clear glass' (Revelation 21:18).

The streets of Sydney are paved with cement and tar but think for a moment of the beauty of heaven. When our Saviour makes the new heavens and earth everything will be perfect. It will be better than anything that you could even begin to imagine.

The new heavens and the new earth are described in the Bible in a way that shows us that God is pure, beautiful, almighty, loving, merciful and gracious. Is a place reserved for you in the new heavens and earth? If you love God and are trusting in Jesus for your salvation, all will be well for you on the day of judgement.

A WHISTLE-STOP TOUR OF AUSTRALIA

The Great Ocean Road

The Great Ocean Road wends its way along the rugged southern Victorian coast. It passes golden sandy beaches, rain forests and farming areas. Along the coast there are limestone pinnacles standing tall in the ocean. Some of these cliffs are well over one hundred metres tall and show the scars of wind and waves.

DESTINATIONS

MR ETERNITY

Sydney is well known for the many great fireworks displays that take place to mark the start of the new year. I'm sure that most people who watched the Sydney Olympic Games, in the year 2000 saw the best fireworks show ever. The company that organises the displays uses the Sydney Harbour Bridge for the most spectacular sections of the show.

When the year 2000 was born and the brilliant colour of the fireworks was about to end, suddenly in perfect 'copperplate' writing there appeared on the bridge the one word *Eternity*.

Most people watching would have been puzzled by that word, but there would have been a few who remembered the name Arthur Stace, a Sydney Christian who made that word famous.

In 1956 a Sydney minister was out walking one night when he spied a man crouched down writing on the footpath.

'Are you Mr Eternity?' he asked.

'Guilty,' came the reply, and at last the mystery of Mr Eternity was solved. For twenty-six years Arthur Stace had spent hours almost every night writing *Eternity* in white chalk on the Sydney footpaths. No one knew who was responsible, until Mr Thompson of a Sydney Baptist church caught Arthur Stace in the act. The word was clearly seen with letters about thirty centimetres in height.

Arthur Stace was born in Sydney in 1884. Both of his parents were drunkards and frequently he slept on a bag under the house in order to escape their fierce beatings. With his brother and sisters he searched for food in garbage tins and often stole bread and milk from local homes. At the age of fifteen he was gaoled for stealing money to buy alcohol, as he had become a drunkard like his parents.

He became a soldier during the first world war and fought in France for some time.

After the war he returned to Sydney and the alcohol, but he wanted to give it up and become a sober man. On 6 August, 1930 he went to a Sydney church because everyone who attended was given a cup of tea and 'rock-cakes' after the service. When he saw the difference between the 'down-and-outs' - and the kindly, well dressed Christians, he said to himself, 'Look at them and look at us. I'm going to have a go at what they have got.' He listened to what the minister preached and heard the gospel for the first time.

Later, to one of his friends he said: 'I went to get a cup of tea and a rock-cake, but I met "the Rock of Ages." He then made his way to a nearby park and sitting under a fig tree, with tears running down his face cried out the simple prayer: 'God be merciful to me, a sinner!'

He began attending church, keeping himself clean and tidy and stopped drinking alcohol. One word that the minister often said in his sermons was *Eternity*. Arthur had only little schooling, but God gave him the ability to write that one word - *Eternity* - in beautiful, copperplate writing. He married, found permanent work and settled down to live a Christian life. However, God called him to a simple task.

He would get out of bed before 4:00 am each morning and set off for a Sydney suburb, where he'd write that one word many times on the footpath. Newspapers soon began to write about the mysterious 'Mr Eternity.' It is estimated that Arthur Stace wrote *Eternity* over half a million times in thirty years - about thirty times each night.

He then began holding gospel meetings on a street corner in Sydney, and everywhere he went he carried a suitcase full of tracts to distribute. During the lunchtime break from his daily work he would go about putting tracts in letter boxes.

Today, the word *Eternity*, made of brass, is to be found in a cement footpath, near the Sydney Opera House. In 1965 the clock bell of the Sydney Post Office was to be replaced and within the huge bell was found the word *Eternity*. Before being hoisted to its place high up in the Post Office tower a crane had for just one night lifted it only a few feet off the ground and Arthur had taken the opportunity to write his word.

Mr Eternity died on 30 June, 1967, aged eighty-three. He had been a faithful disciple of the Lord Jesus who had saved him those many years before. That one word *Eternity* was used by God to make people think about preparing for judgement and eternity in heaven or hell. The converted thief and drunkard, 'Mr Eternity,' had for all those years given his time and energy to witness about the Lord Jesus Christ - just a one word witness. We read in Ecclesiastes 3:11 - 'He [God] has made everything beautiful in its time. Also he has put *Eternity* in their hearts.'

Have you prepared to spend *Eternity* with the Saviour, the Lord Jesus Christ?

A WHISTLE-STOP TOUR OF AUSTRALIA

London Bridge

Further along the Great Ocean Road is a place called 'The London Bridge.' Years ago there was a tall limestone cliff connected to a towering pinnacle out from the shore. The wind and waves had worn away the lower region leaving a 'bridge' formation between both places. It was possible for people to walk across the pinnacle out from the shore. However, in 1990 a couple visiting the 'London Bridge' walked across only to see the walkway collapse into the ocean behind them. A helicopter had to be called up to rescue them.

KING'S CROSS

Sydney is well known for the suburb 'Kings Cross.' It was once known as 'Queen's Cross,' no doubt named after Queen Victoria. Following her death the region was called King's Cross as the Empire then had a King. The name 'Cross' came about because three wide, busy roads intersected there.

King's Cross has a bad reputation. It is not safe at night as criminal gangs cause problems for the police and the people who live in the area. Quite frequently King's Cross is mentioned on the TV news, usually not for good reasons. However, if you like Chinese food King's Cross is the place to go.

Around the shopping centre there are many areas of beautiful houses that I couldn't afford to purchase. Gardens are well kept and the flowers are like a multicoloured carpet.

It is the name - King's Cross - that turns my attention to the King of kings, and Lord of lords, Jesus Christ.

Death on the cross was very painful and cruel, and Roman law said that no Roman citizen who was sentenced to death was to die that way. Usually they were beheaded.

Our Saviour was put to death by crucifixion on a Roman cross. This means that there truly was a King's cross! When the Lord was nailed on it he carried our sins. He must have looked like just any other criminal that day when he died. The King of the Jews hung upon a cross. There he was forsaken by his Father and experienced hell for all of his people. He gave his life as a sacrifice for sin! He died for me. Did he die for you?

The King's cross was made from wood and Christ was secured to that cross by nails through his hands and his feet. The rough Roman soldiers had whipped him and taken his clothes. My Saviour was naked upon the cross. The One who was God had humbled himself to the point of death so that his people might live with him eternally. We are told to look 'unto Jesus, the author and finisher of our faith, who for the joy that was set before him endured the cross, despising the shame, and has sat down at the right hand of the throne of God' (Hebrews 12:2). The sinless, willing Jesus felt the pain of the cross and was forsaken by God, all for the sake of his people. If there had not been a King's cross in Jerusalem those many years ago no one would be saved and everyone would be sentenced to eternal hell.

I pray that you personally know the King who died upon that Roman cross.

A WHISTLE-STOP TOUR OF AUSTRALIA

Echidna

This is also called the Spiny Ant eater. It has a curved backbone and a back which is covered with strong, sharp spines. Adults have been known to grow to fifty centimetres in size and they can live for over thirty-five years.

God designed these creatures so that they can easily defend themselves. Not only do the spines drive off any attackers the Echidna also has a razor-sharp spur on its hind legs. This spur can severely wound any animal foolish enough to attack.

BEWARE OF
SUBMARINES!

Australia has never experienced war such as happened in Europe and Asia, but 188 Japanese planes bombed Darwin, the capital city of Northern Territory on 19 February, 1942. This attack resulted in the death of 243 people, sank eight ships and destroyed planes, homes and military installations. Several other areas were bombed by the invading forces with further loss of life. Australia feared an invasion of Japanese forces, which, thank God, never happened.

Sydney, also experienced attacks but this time from submarines. They were seeking out ships to destroy in the Pacific Ocean. On 30 May, 1942 a large 'mother submarine' launched off a sea plane which flew over Sydney without anyone noticing. This plane was attempting to find targets for the midget submarines that would later enter Sydney Harbour secretly. Those small submarines were carried on the larger mother submarine, held in place by metal clamps.

On 8 June, 1942 one of the mother submarines came close to the Sydney coast during the night. It had intended to destroy the Sydney Harbour Bridge, but its shells landed in the coastal suburbs causing minor damage. Only one shell exploded, but no one was killed. At 8 p.m. a midget submarine was detected in the Harbour, but when it became entangled in an anti submarine net the crew blew it up before it could be captured.

A couple of hours later a second midget submarine entered the Harbour. This time it was detected, but no one took any notice as it was thought to be a small ship moving about. At 10:27 pm it was realised that the submarine was an enemy one and all ships were notified to be on guard. The American battleship USS Chicago opened fire on the submarine. A second submarine entered the Harbour, only this time it was spotted by several naval vessels that attempted to ram it, after dropping depth charges.

One of the midget submarines fired two torpedoes at the USS Chicago, one exploding beside a ferry killing nineteen sailors. One of the shells fired from the American ship hit 'Pinchgut Island.' The spot where the shell hit the island tower can still be seen.

The small submarines were finally dragged from the harbour and the dead Japanese sailors were given a suitable burial. The submarines are now on display in Canberra.

In James 4:1-2 we read: 'What causes fights and quarrels among you? Don't they come from your desires that battle within you? You want something but don't get it. You kill and covet, but you cannot have what you want. You quarrel and fight.' (NIV)

Wars start because a country has something another country wants. So often if they can't get what they want in a peaceful way, they fight to obtain it.

There is one fight in which you all should be involved. The apostle Paul wrote to his dear friend Timothy: 'But you, O man of God, flee these things and pursue righteousness, godliness, faith, love, patience, gentleness. Fight the good fight of faith, lay hold on eternal life, to which you were also called and have confessed the good confession in the presence of many witnesses' (1 Timothy 6:11-12). Timothy was a godly young man and he was told by Paul to look at the Christian life as a lifelong battle which he must win. He had to fight against all the devil's temptations. He had to love God instead of the world.

Paul wrote, telling Timothy, 'I have fought the good fight, I have finished the race, I have kept the faith' (2 Timothy 4:7). Paul had remained faithful to his God and Saviour, always teaching the truth. He had fought on in many difficult situations, but at last was nearing the end of his life - his race was almost over.

We must do all we can to avoid becoming involved in senseless squabbles with other people, but live a peaceful life, which is one mark of being a Christian. Jesus said: 'Blessed are the peacemakers, for they shall be called sons of God' (Matthew 5:9).

Is this you? Do you endeavour to live in peace?

A WHISTLE-STOP TOUR OF AUSTRALIA

The Great Barrier Reef

This colourful underwater garden is built by billions of small sea creatures called polyps. In addition to the 400 species of polyps, there are over 2,500 categories of fish and 200 bird varieties living along the reef. There are 400 categories of molluscs, fifteen species of snakes and 500 varieties of seaweed.

Australia's Great Barrier Reef stretches over 2,000 kilometres along the coast of New South Wales and Queensland.

The Australian government has established the 'Great Barrier Reef Marine Park,' which is responsible for ensuring the reef maintains its pristine condition.

SYDNEY HARBOUR

In Sydney's early days there was just one way to carry passengers from one side of the harbour to the other and that was by boat. Later large ferries were built and sailed regularly from the northern side to the southern side. When gale force winds are blowing and the waves are rather big, the ferries can't run - it is simply too dangerous for the sailors and passengers.

To make life easier and provide a quick way across the harbour, a bridge was built which has been given the nickname - 'the Coat Hanger.' The New South Wales Government didn't have the money to build the huge bridge and borrowed what was needed from the British Government. To cross the bridge motorists pay a toll and this money is used to keep the bridge in good repair. The painters just keep painting. When they finish painting the bridge they start all over again.

A third way to cross the harbour is by a newly opened tunnel. Again motorists must pay a toll to use the tunnel, but it is a quick way of getting from one side to the other.

So you can cross the harbour by ferry, bridge or tunnel but the best known of the three ways to cross the harbour is by the Sydney Harbour Bridge. Every year the world is able to watch the finest fireworks display marking the start of the new year with the bridge being the centre of activities. The Harbour is surrounded by a multitude of colours for several hours as the people say 'Good bye' to the old year and, 'Welcome!' to the new one. Hundreds of boats are on the Harbour and their bright lights, with the reflection of the colours from the fireworks make the water an amazing mixture of sparkling colour.

The apostle Paul wrote that the Lord Jesus has a special role in the Christian's life. We read his words: 'For there is one God and one Mediator between

God and men, the Man Christ Jesus...' (1 Timothy 2:5). Despite what some churches teach, Paul has very clearly said that if we want to approach God we must do so through the only Mediator provided, and that is Jesus Christ. Jesus had already taught this truth when he said: 'I am the way, the truth, and the life. No one comes to the Father except through Me' (John 14:6).

Mediators are the 'go betweens.' Just as Sydney Harbour Bridge is a go between from one side of the harbour to the other, the Lord Jesus is the go between or mediator between mankind and God.

The bridge, tunnel and ferries show me that we are able to build ways of crossing the harbour without getting wet.

And this also reminds me of another story from the Bible. In the book of Exodus Moses and the citizens of Israel escaped from the land of Egypt and arrived at the Red Sea. The Egyptian army was coming to destroy them and in front of the people was a wide expanse of water.

God told Moses to hold out Aaron's staff over the sea. When he did, a wind came up and separated the water so that the Israelites could walk across on dry land.

Our God is all powerful! It is only by the grace of God that we can ever enter his presence, and that is through his Son, the Lord Jesus Christ.

We have a glorious God!

A WHISTLE-STOP TOUR OF AUSTRALIA

The Coat Hanger - Sydney Harbour Bridge

As your plane approaches Sydney airport, you should see the Sydney Harbour Bridge, affectionately called 'The Coat Hanger'. It is the largest steel arched bridge in the world. It's total length, including the roadway is 1,149 metres. The top of the arch is 134 metres above sea level. Painting the bridge uses 270,000 litres of paint. When building the bridge 58,000 tonnes of steel were used and 6,000,000 steel rivets. Tourists can, for a price, walk over the archway which will provide those who are not scared of heights some great photo opportunities.

DON'T LAUGH
TOO LOUD

In Sydney there are special parks set aside for everyone to have a very happy time. The best known one is 'Luna Park' which is situated on the northern harbour shore, near the northern pylon of the Sydney Harbour Bridge. This park was opened in 1935. It is a fun park and when everyone leaves they do so talking about the exciting day they had.

The day starts with people making their way through a huge, laughing mouth. There is the 'ghost' train ride which takes you through a very dark tunnel that has a lot of crazy faces and funny looking animals that jump out at the passengers on the train. There is a lot of screaming and laughing coming from the people on the train.

From a very big ferris wheel you are able to see over the harbour. I don't like having my feet off the ground and have never had the ride, but my family members say it's a great thrill.

There are other places where you can win prizes if you throw a ball and knock down the target. The park also has an area where you can drive a 'dodgem car' around a circular track. That is really good fun!

One year Luna Park had a special time when all rides and other activities were free if you could hand in a plastic lid from a tub of butter upon which was written 'Free rides at Luna Park.'

The children in my class at school collected over one hundred lids for me and I took the family to Sydney for a fun day.

We had a great time and returned home very weary. Luna Park is a very popular spot for the people of Sydney - and for tourists who come to the New South Wales capital city for a few days.

The word 'laugh' doesn't appear many times in the Bible, but we read in Psalm 2 about a humorous situation. The Psalmist creates a picture of humans who think they are so powerful that they can totally ignore God. They reckon that he is not powerful enough to defeat them.

Then we read 'The One enthroned in heaven laughs; the Lord scoffs at them' (Psalm 2:4 (NIV)).

God laughs at the stupidity of men and women who think they can do as they please as if God didn't exist.

Just imagine that you've found an ant that can talk. Now this ant is really rather stupid. He is a very tiny ant and he is looking at a huge elephant standing before him. The little ant flexes his muscles and says, 'I can defeat you! Look at my great muscles.'

If elephants could laugh and if the elephant could see the ant in the first place it wouldn't be surprising if he laughed out loud!

Our God is all powerful. In Psalm 2 we are told that God has established his Son as King of his nation. That nation consists of all people who have repented of their sins and are trusting the Lord Jesus for their salvation.

The Psalm concludes with the words: 'Kiss the Son, lest he be angry, and you perish in the way, when his wrath is kindled but a little. Blessed are all those who put their trust in Him' (Psalm 2:12).

There is only one way of finding peace with God and that is through Christ, the Saviour of his people.

Have you made peace with God - or are you living like that silly ant believing that you can live as you please and never face judgement?

A WHISTLE-STOP TOUR OF AUSTRALIA

Luna Park

Luna Park was formerly occupied by a series of workshops, cranes, and railway sidings used to provide for the construction of the Sydney Harbour Bridge. When the Harbour Bridge was completed in 1932, North Sydney Council opened applications for tenders to develop the site. Herman Phillips won the tender in March, 1935. The construction and assembly costs amounted to £60,000, and 1,000 engineers, structural workers, fitters, and artists were employed to complete the task. As of 2006, Sydney's Luna Park is open and operating, having celebrated its 70th anniversary in October 2005 and is now the largest amusement park in New South Wales.

THE SYDNEY OPERA HOUSE

Almost every person enjoys singing. In the Bible we read many times of people singing. In the Old Testament we read of the Israelites singing Psalms in their worship. In the New Testament James wrote in his epistle: 'Is anyone among you suffering? Let him pray. Is anyone cheerful? Let him sing psalms' (James 5:13).

We read that in heaven God is praised in songs. In Revelation 5:9-10 we read: 'And they sang a new song, saying: 'You are worthy to take the scroll, and to open its seals; for you were slain, and have redeemed us to God by your blood out of every tribe and tongue and people and nation, and have made us kings and priests to our God; and we shall reign on the earth.' Singing is a natural and wonderful way to praise our God. On earth many people complain that they don't have good voices for singing, but in heaven the saints will sing in perfect voices.

Now in Sydney we have one of the twenty one wonders of the modern world - the Sydney Opera House. A competition is being held and on New Year's Day, 2007 the best seven man made wonders of the world will be announced. At present the Opera House is number twelve in the list. It was in the year 200 BC that the first seven wonders of the world was established.

The Sydney Opera House is known throughout the world as an amazing structure. It was officially opened by Queen Elizabeth II on 20 October, 1973.

Its design was to give the impression of sails which fit perfectly into the harbour setting. The structure is found at Bennnelong Point which was named after an aboriginal who became a friend of Governor Phillip. The building cost over a billion dollars to construct and is used by the best singers and choirs in the world. However, the best songs of praise that can be heard in the Opera House are weak when compared to the choir of voices heard in Paradise praising God.

Several years ago there was a 'news flash' that the Opera House had begun to sink into the harbour waters. It was claimed that in one year the foundations had sunk by about fifteen centimetres. The news reader said that there was nothing that could be done to prevent the sinking and that within fifty or so years, water would flood the great hall. Most people were surprised that the majestic building was in serious trouble - until we realised it was 1 April!

The magnificent building is visited by many millions of people every year. Thousands buy costly tickets to see and hear operas being performed, and plays acted. What joy it is to sing praises to God, here on earth but more so when we enter heaven!

A WHISTLE-STOP TOUR OF AUSTRALIA

The Opera House

The Opera House is not far from Sydney Harbour Bridge. It has been built on Bennelong Point. The Opera House was completed in 1973 at a cost of $102, 000, 000 and it took sixteen years to complete. The outside structure is covered with over one million tiles. The roof is held together with 350 kilometres of steel cable. There are 1,000 rooms inside The Opera House and a lot of work has gone into making sure the acoustics are as near perfect as possible. Each year there are approximately 3,000 different events held here.

DESTINATIONS

THE YACHT RACE

Sydney is known throughout the world for two racing events. The first is the Sydney - Hobart sailing race, that attracts boats from many overseas entrants. The glory comes not just from winning the race, but from crossing the finishing line.

The race starts in Sydney Harbour on Boxing day and yachts from ten to thirty metres in length make their way through the Port Jackson Heads, turn south and set sail for Hobart, the capital city of Tasmania, a distance of 630 nautical miles. Those involved in the race spend many months preparing their boats. There is no rule which limits the size and number of sails used. This means many sails must be correctly rolled up and packed away, all the reels greased and a good deal of time is spent polishing the hull to make it slide through the water at the fastest speed.

Sydney Harbour is a mass of coloured boats on Boxing Day as the yachts sail about, making sure they don't cross the starting line before the starting gun is fired. It is estimated that there are about 400,000 men, women and children in their boats and along the harbour shore to get the best possible view of the great event. Another 700,000 have their eyes glued to the television to see the start of the race. It is an exciting day for everyone! Many wives, husbands and friends, after watching the yachts get underway, travel to the airport to catch a plane for Hobart, where they will welcome the sailors after the long haul south.

Originally the yacht race started in Sydney on Boxing Day to end in Hobart on or about New Year's day. However with the modern boats available these days the race now just lasts anything from abotu two to three days. It is interesting to realise that the first race that took place in 1945 lasted six days.

Every boat carries sufficient food and water for their time at sea and all boats are equipped with the latest computerised charts which are used to plot the exact route that will be sailed. Each boat carries electronic location beacons and lights in case of an accident and help is needed. In strong winds some of the sailing ships travel at speeds of up to thirty knots. To rescue a sailor who has fallen overboard, means time is wasted as the yacht has to turn back and find the person. All sailors wear life jackets and most wear a harness connected to the boat. However, if a sailor falls overboard during gale force winds and rough seas he is often pulled aboard dead, having drowned.

In most boats the winches that are used to control the sails and masts are not worked by hand, but by an engine that is kept running all the time. Some of the largest boats get their best speed in strong winds, which means that the bow of the boat is on one swell and the stern is riding the following ocean swell. The long flat hull is then out of the water. This can mean that the fin which has a large, heavy bulb attached is suspended in the air. These bulbs weigh as much as twenty-five tonnes and in rough seas can cause the ship to break apart. This has in fact once happened. When the ship's captain saw the hull splitting apart, the sailors immediately took down the sails and slowly made their way to the nearest harbour. Another ship had its keel broken off! The boat then rolled over as the crew quickly scrambled into the life rafts.

In 1998 six sailors and five boats were lost in the huge storm that swept across the pathway of the ships. Usually however, the forecast is for good weather and all boats and sailors arrive safely in the Hobart harbour where they are given a great, colourful welcome from the thousands who have gathered there. Many wives, husbands and friends of the sailors are waiting ready to hug and praise their loved ones as they come ashore. Last year (2005) the weather was so good that the winning yacht beat the record by more than one hour.

The first Sydney-Hobart sailing race was held in 1945 by some war weary soldiers. The race has grown in the number of competitors, but the most important thing about the race is to complete the course. This was what Jesus said about his life of obedience to his Father: 'I have glorified you on the earth. I have finished the work which you have given me to do' (John 17:4). That is why Jesus shouted out on the cross: 'It is finished!' (John 19:30). His work of salvation was completed.

All who call themselves Christians must persevere and finish the course. We must be able to say with the apostle Paul: 'I have fought the good fight, I have finished the race, I have kept the faith.' Paul then spoke of his reward: 'Finally, there is laid up for me the crown of righteousness, which the Lord, the righteous Judge, will give to me on that Day, and not to me only but also to all who have loved his appearing' (2 Timothy 4:7,8).

A WHISTLE-STOP TOUR OF AUSTRALIA

The Twelve Apostles

Along the Great Ocean Road is a group of towering rock formations called 'The Twelve Apostles'. It is not possible to see all twelve limestone formations from the one spot, but there are now only ten of the twelve pinnacles still standing. Gale force winds and huge waves have caused the cliff faces to collapse into the ocean.

DESTINATIONS

THE CITY TO SURF
FOOT RACE

This race attracts the attention of the best distance runners in the world. The starting line is in central Sydney and the finishing tape is at Bondi Beach, a distance of fourteen kilometres. The first such race was held in 1971 and is now an annual event. Steve Moneghetti holds the record for the distance, that being 40:03 minutes.

The start of the race is an amazing sight as about 50,000 competitors crowd around waiting to hear the starting gun fired. It is not only athletes who take part in the event, but women with children in strollers set off slowly, usually giving up after a short time. The competitors range from youngsters to aged men and women. Every competitor is given a number and their time is accurately recorded if they finish the course. The day after the race a city newspaper carries the list of competitors in the order they finished, and with the times taken. One of the steep hills that must be conquered along the way is called 'Heartbreak Hill,' as that is the stretch of the race where many give up.

Some fail to complete the course because they become ill and receive medical treatment from paramedics on the scene. There are quite a lot of competitors who take the race seriously and spend many months training for the event. They not only want to complete the distance, they also want to win the race. They run daily for long distances and exercise every muscle in their body in preparation for the gruelling event.

On the day of the race the police close streets so that the runners have no danger from traffic. Along the way the runners are able to grab a flask of water to drink to ensure they do not suffer from dehydration.

Try and imagine those 50,000 competitors dressed in many colours spread out over several kilometres as they make their way towards the finishing line. Thousands of people line the streets watching and cheering. I'm one of those lazy people who sit down in front of the TV to watch the event, but I still find the race very exciting.

The City to Surf foot race is like the Christian life which is a race where completion is of all importance. The apostle Paul in his letter to the Philippians wrote of God who commenced a saving work in the heart of a sinner. He wrote that he was 'confident of this very thing, that he who has begun a good work in you will complete it until the day of Jesus Christ' (Philippians 1:6).

Likewise Jesus gave his people the assurance when he said: 'My sheep hear my voice, and I know them, and they follow me. And I give them eternal life, and they shall never perish; neither shall anyone snatch them out of my hand. My Father, who has given them to me, is greater than all; and no one is able to snatch them out of my Father's hand' (John 10:27-29).

If we belong to Christ we will successfully complete the Christian race as Jesus has hold of his people and will never let them go. Hallelujah!

A WHISTLE-STOP TOUR OF AUSTRALIA

Bondi Beach

Australia is a nation well known for its surfing community and beaches. Bondi Beach (pronounced "Bond-eye") is a popular beach in Sydney, Australia. It is situated roughly seven kilometres from the centre of the city. Large numbers of tourists visit Bondi Beach throughout the year, and many Irish and British tourists spend Christmas Day there. There are five strong rip currents around Bondi beach one being known as the "Backpackers Express". There is an underwater shark net shared, during the summer months, with other beaches along the southern part of the coast. Bondi Beach is the end point of the City to Surf Foot Race which is held each year in August.

THE EASTER SHOW

Each year a two week show is held in Sydney at Easter time - the Royal Easter Show. Australia in some ways is a huge farm, and this was especially so in the first 150 years of European settlement. Many countries today purchase our wheat, beef, lamb, fish, lobsters, prawns, fruit and vegetables.

Early in our history 'Junior Farmers' Clubs' were formed to encourage young men and women to become farmers. Soon after, agricultural shows became popular where prizes were awarded for the best crops and animals. A popular section of the exhibits was the cooking where the most delicious cakes were displayed. There was also a section for sewing. Much time was spent setting out each Club's displays which attracted the attention of almost every person who attended the shows.

Eventually the decision was made to have a Sydney Show where the best produce from all regions could be displayed with prizes awarded. Special awards were made annually to members of the Junior Farmers' Clubs who excelled. For some it meant an overseas trip to study farming in foreign countries.

In the vegetable section some of the vegetables are huge. The winning pumpkin is sometimes the size of three or four pillows. And the cooking section has only the very best! Those delicious chocolate cakes make the onlookers' mouths water.

Displays are not only of fruit and vegetables, but farm animals also. Owners wash and brush their animals, clip tails, polish hooves, clip away unsightly hair and sometimes plait their horses' manes. Gaining a first prize usually means that farmers can ask big prices for the sale of the winning animal or their offspring. The show has grown and now there are displays of farming equipment and many other exhibits of interest.

On one of the most important show days there is the 'Grand Parade.' Here the prize winning animals wearing sashes indicating their awards, are paraded around the show ring to the cheers and clapping from onlookers. The Royal Easter Show is the largest of its kind in Australia and the sixth largest in the world. During the last few years over one million people have visited the show to see the state's best produce.

School classes often visit the show to learn about farming. Many city children have little knowledge about the food they eat. To some, milk comes in plastic containers, purchased from a supermarket. The production of milk is a mystery to them. The New South Wales Education Department closes schools for one day so children can attend the show.

One of the most exciting places for youngsters is 'Side-show alley.' Here many people have a ride on the huge ferris wheel which gently spins high into the sky giving a wonderful view of Sydney. Younger boys and girls, sometimes with their mums and dads standing beside them enjoy a ride on the Merry-go-round. Of course there are those terrifying rides that bring screams of fright from even the bravest person strapped to a seat. There are the 'Knock-'em-down' stalls where prizes are given if you can knock down a target.

The sheep dog trials are really interesting. The shepherd stands and gives directions to his dog either by calling or whistling - sometimes with hand movements. The dog then rounds up some sheep and drives them into an enclosure. These well trained dogs know that the shortest way from one side of the mob of sheep to the other side is across the backs of the animals. It is amazing to see the sheep dog running across the flock of sheep. The dog that completes the task in the shortest time is the winner.

Australia is known for its specially bred 'Blue Heeler' cattle dog. They are a greyish blue colour, and know that to make a cow or bull move, a nip on the heels brings results. As well as moving, the animals sometimes kick. However the wise dog knows how to escape being hurt; they drop down flat on the ground, and the animal's hooves go over them.

Everyone pays to enter the show as do the exhibitors and it is this money that in part is used to pay the prizes. Some big companies also award prizes, knowing that this is a good way of advertising their produce.

To win a prize means a lot of work preparing the exhibit.

The apostle Paul entered the Christian race, serving the Lord Jesus. He saw his sinful nature and knew he needed a Saviour. This salvation didn't require him to do anything. He wrote an important truth to the Ephesian Christians that you and I need to believe: 'For by grace you have been saved through faith, and that not of yourselves; it is the gift of God, not of works, lest anyone should boast' (Ephesians 2:8,9). We don't earn our salvation like the owner of the cow earns first prize - through a lot of hard work. Our salvation is God's free gift. Having received the gift of saving faith in Jesus Christ we then commence a life of obedience to his commands. Paul wrote 'we are his workmanship, created in Christ Jesus for good works, which God prepared beforehand that we should walk in them' (Ephesians 2:10).

Don't ever think that God saves you because you are a nice, kind person!

A WHISTLE-STOP TOUR OF AUSTRALIA

Agriculture is a large part of Australian life. Australia is famous for its Merino sheep but also for its sheepdogs. Merino sheep wool is tightly crimped and springy and unlike "traditional" wool, it is much finer, softer, and, best of all, itch-free. The Kelpie is an Australian sheep dog that is great at herding and droving. The breed is energetic with a high level of endurance. It can drive a mob of sheep over sixty kilometres in extreme conditions. Working Kelpies are renowned for running along the backs of sheep when moving them through chutes.

DESTINATIONS

THE CENTREPOINT TOWER

There is a place in Sydney where you can eat a really good meal three hundred metres above street level. You might not want to imagine what it would be like to be in an earthquake but if one was to hit Sydney we are told that the tower is the safest building in Sydney because of its special construction.

The building is made from reinforced concrete and held upright by fifty-six steel cables, each approximately 182 metres in length. The tower naturally sways in the wind, but is constructed in such a way that its movement is only slight. Those who planned the tower have made use of tanks of water on the roof to prevent extreme swaying.

Centrepoint Tower was built in central Sydney in 1981 and is the city's tallest building. During its first year 1.3 million people took the trip by lift to the top. There is a stairwell in case of an emergency, but very few people struggle to the top climbing the stairs. My daughters gave me a birthday meal at the restaurant at the top so I could see Sydney from the Centrepoint lookout. I don't like heights and refused to sit beside the window. I believed I could feel the swaying caused by the wind. The meal was delicious, but I was pleased to get my feet once again on solid ground.

The top portion of the tower slowly revolves so during a meal one is able to see all of Sydney from the nearby ocean and harbour region to the far distant Blue Mountains.

A recent addition to the tower is a glass flooring built outside at the top. Of course there's a safety railing around the area and everyone who dares to step outside, after paying to do so, must wear special clothing and some harness to make sure they don't slip and fall from the glass flooring. The glass is very strong, but is clear and to look down must be frightening. The cars far below look so small and the people are like ants moving about.

All things considered Centrepoint Tower is a very safe building, providing the best views of the Sydney area and a place many people want to visit.

Christians have a place they want to visit and in which they want to live forever - that is the new heavens and new earth that Christ will make. This will be the eternal home for the saints of all ages. Saving faith in the Saviour is the one and only entrance to Christ's Paradise, which will be a home of perfect safety for all its citizens.

The apostle John wrote of the wonder of the new home for God's people: 'And I heard a loud voice from heaven saying, "Behold, the tabernacle of God is with men, and he will dwell with them, and they shall be his people. God himself will be with them and be their God. And God will wipe away every tear from their eyes; there shall be no more death, nor sorrow, nor crying. There shall be no more pain, for the former things have passed away."'

A WHISTLE-STOP TOUR OF AUSTRALIA

Centrepoint Tower

Sydney Tower (also known as the AMP Tower, AMP Centrepoint Tower, Centrepoint Tower or just Centrepoint) is Sydney's tallest free-standing structure, and the second tallest in Australia (with the Q1 building on the Gold Coast being the tallest). The tower stands 305 metres above the central business district, it is located at 100 Market Street, and sits upon Centrepoint (to which the tower is often referred), an office building and shopping centre. The tower is open to the public, and is one of the most prominent tourist attractions in the city, being visible from a number of vantage points throughout town and from adjoining suburbs.

DESTINATIONS

THE SYDNEY ZOO

When you visit Sydney you should make every effort to spend a day at the Taronga Park Zoo where you will see one of the world's greatest collection of animals. The zoo is built on one of the most picturesque foreshores of the Sydney Harbour. To get to the park is easy - you either drive your car to a parking area beside the front entrance, or catch a ferry which allows you to pass through the lower level entrance.

Having arrived you set about walking the miles of wide pathways, seeing animals from all parts of the earth. The animals, birds and fish are kept in areas made to look like the places from which the animals come. The polar bears have icy cold water while the camels have a warm enclosure which makes them feel at home. Many millions of dollars have been spent building a zoo that is considered to be the best in the world.

The birds have large cages and the fish swim in huge aquariums. You can see a great variety of reptiles and spiders and as you walk about you will come face to face with some gentle animals that walk along the pathways hoping to be given something delicious to eat. Each time you visit the zoo you will return home with a special story to tell about your day.

I took one of my classes for a day at the zoo. Several parents, one a minister's wife, came along with me to make sure no one was eaten by a lion. The most exciting part of that zoo visit was when we reached the gorilla cage. The very large gorilla was looking at the humans who were looking and laughing at him. Maybe he didn't like the laughter as he suddenly bent over and grabbed a handful of grass and manure. Then looking at the laughing class he took aim and threw the foul mess straight at the minister's wife. The poor lady's clothes stank for the rest of the day. She eventually bought a raincoat which she wore to hide her messy, smelly clothes. I know that that incident was the most exciting part of our visit to the zoo - every child mentioned it in their excursion report.

One unusual Australian animal is the platypus. It has webbed feet like a duck, a strong broad tail and a soft, rubbery bill for a nose and mouth. The platypus and the echidna are mammals, but are the only mammals in the world that lay eggs.

The platypus digs burrows in the banks of the creek, and in them lays its eggs and hatches its young. The baby platypus then sucks milk from some hairs attached to the glands from which milk oozes. After about six weeks the babies have grown sufficiently to be allowed to leave the nest and start searching for food at the bed of the creeks. After about four months the babies are weaned. They then live on worms, insects, crustaceans, molluscs, tadpoles, the larvae of caddis flies, mayflies, two-winged flies and shrimps. They carry their prey to the surface of the water in cheek-pouches where they are eaten.

Australia's colonists sent a stuffed duckbilled, web-footed platypus to London's British Museum.

The scientists thought it was a 'fake' animal that had been made by the colonists by putting parts of various animals together. They tried to pull the stuffed animal apart, but couldn't do so and came to the conclusion that it was one of the world's strangest animals.

When you walk through a zoo and see all the creatures, remember that they were made by God. The apostle John writes of Christ's part in the creation: 'All things were made through him, and without him nothing was made that was made' (John 1:3). The apostle Paul wrote of the creation and Christ: 'For by Him all things were created that are in heaven and that are on earth, visible and invisible, whether thrones or dominions or principalities or powers. All things were created through Him and for him' (Colossians 1:16).

As you look about at all you can see, remember that it was God who created all things. What a most powerful and wise God we have!

A WHISTLE-STOP TOUR OF AUSTRALIA

Taronga Zoo

This is the city zoo of Sydney and was officially opened on October 7th, 1916. It is located on the shores of Sydney Harbour in Mosman. Taronga Zoo is home to over 26,000 animals on 287 hectares, making it one of the largest of its kind. The first public zoo in New South Wales opened in 1884 at Billy Goat Swamp in Moore Park. After realising that the Moore Park site was too small, the NSW Government granted forty-three acres of land north of Sydney Harbour. A further nine acres were later granted in 1916. In February, 2003 Taronga Zoo became the second zoo in Australia to breed the platypus.

A MAP OF
SYDNEY

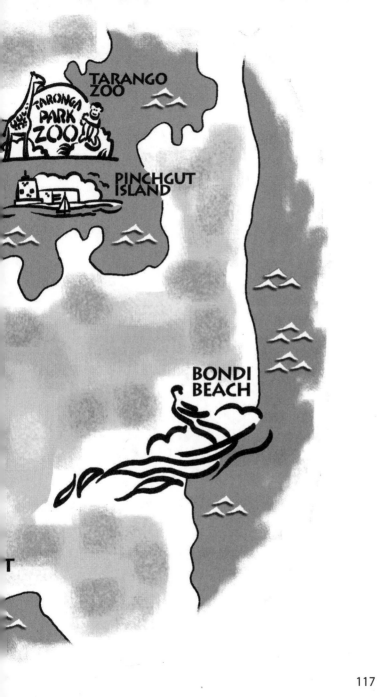

TARANGO
ZOO

TARONGA
PARK
ZOO

PINCHGUT
ISLAND

BONDI
BEACH

T

A TRAVELLER'S BIBLE STUDY

It's good to pick a theme or a topic and see what the Bible has to say about it.

Here are seven different themes for you to look up in the Word of God if you are travelling to Sydney or even just staying at home.

1. God is with me

Genesis 28:15
Joshua 1:9
Psalm 139:18
Matthew 28:20

Exodus 33:14
Psalm 73:23
Zephaniah 3:15

2. The Lord is in control

Matthew 28:18
John 3:35
Hebrews 7:25
Nahum 1:3

John 17:2
Ephesians 1:22
Psalm 62:11

3. God knows everything

Joshua 22:22
Psalm 44:21
Daniel 2:22

1 Samuel 2:3
Psalm 103:14
Matthew 6:8

2 Timothy 2:19

4. The whole world belongs to God

Psalm 9:8   Psalm 24:1
Psalm 33:8   Psalm 89:11
Psalm 93:1   Acts 17:24
Romans 3:19

5. God is the Creator

Genesis 1:1   Psalm 51:10
Psalm 102:18   Romans 8:22
Colossians 1:16   1 Timothy 4:4
Revelation 4:11

6. God is my Creator

Genesis 1:26   Psalm 139:13
Ecclesiastes 12:1   Matthew 25:34
2 Corinthians 5:17   Ephesians 1:4
1 Peter 4:19

7. The Lord is Saviour

2 Samuel 22:47   Psalm 18:46
Psalm 25:5   Psalm 42:11
Isaiah 43:11   Luke 2:11
Philippians 3:20

A QUIZ OF AUSTRALIA

1. Who founded Sydney in 1788?

2. How far is Sydney from London?

3. What is Australia's highest mountain?

4. What did Britain do with prisoners when the USA gained independence?

5. What is 'the cat o' nine tails'?

6. What are the wages of sin?

7. What stream ran through the convict settlement and still exists today?

8. Over how many varieties of Kangaroo are there in Australia?

9. Who built the first town along the shores of Sydney Harbour?

10. In Amos chapter 8 what sort of famine did God send?

11. What was the name of the convict who was granted his freedom in order to farm?

12. What unusual thing can an Australian sheepdog do to round up sheep?

13. How many fingers does a Koala have?

14. How did Pinchgut Island get its name?

15. Who was Australia's first bush ranger?

16. Name two things an Emu can't do?

17. What happened in Sydney for the first time on 3rd February 1788?

18. What was the real name of Mr. Eternity?

19. What did he pray under the fig tree?

20. Name two places mentioned in the book where there is or was a King's Cross.

21. What is another name for a Spiny Ant Eater?

22. Who did Jesus say would be called the Sons of God?

23. How long is the Great Barrier Reef?

24. What is the nickname for the Sydney Harbour Bridge?

25. How many tiles cover the Sydney Opera House?

26. On what day does the Sydney-Hobart Yacht Race start?

27. Where does the City to Surf Foot Race end?

28. What sporting event did Sydney host in the year 2000?

29. Is salvation an award for good works?

30. Where can you eat a meal at 300 metres above street level?

Answers:

1. Governor Arthur Phillip
2. 17, 200 Kilometres.
3. Mount Kosciusko.
4. Shipped them to Australia.
5. A whip.
6. Death.
7. Tank Stream.
8. Over 60.
9. The convicts.
10. A famine of his word.
11. James Ruse.
12. It runs across the backs of the sheep.
13. Five.
14. The prisoners on the island were often hungry.
15. John Caesar.
16. Fly and walk backwards.
17. A church service.
18. Arthur Stace.
19. God be merciful to me a sinner.
20. Sydney and Jerusalem.
21. An Echidna.
22. The Peacemakers.

23. Over 2000 kilometres.

24. The Coathanger.

25. 1 million.

26. Boxing day.

27. Bondi Beach.

28. The Olympic games.

29. No. It is a free gift from God.

30. The Centrepoint Tower.

Great Barrier Reef Adventures
Back-packers and tourists flock to Australia,
especially to the amazing Great Barrier Reef.
The water is crystal clear and the fish and sea
creatures are every colour of the rainbow. The
coral beds heave with creatures of every shape
and size, beautiful ones, ugly ones and even
dangerous ones. God has made them all for a
reason.

ISBN 13: 978-1-84550-068-9
1-84550-068-7

Outback Adventures

Australia's Outback is one of the most exciting and adventurous places you can visit. There are so many wide-open spaces, such stunning scenery, amazing animals - and it was all made by God for us to enjoy and look after. Jim Cromarty tells us many interesting facts about this incredible country and shows us how we can also learn about God when we think of his creation.

ISBN 13: 978-1-85792-974-4
1-85792-974-8

CHRISTIAN FOCUS PUBLICATIONS

Christian Focus Publications publishes books for adults and children under its three main imprints: Christian Focus, Mentor and Christian Heritage. Our books reflect that God's word is reliable and Jesus is the way to know him, and live for ever with him.

Our children's publication list includes a Sunday school curriculum that covers pre-school to early teens; puzzle and activity books. We also publish personal and family devotional titles, biographies and inspirational stories that children will love.

If you are looking for quality Bible teaching for children then we have an excellent range of Bible story and age specific theological books.

From pre-school to teenage fiction, we have it covered!

Find us at our web page:
www.christianfocus.com